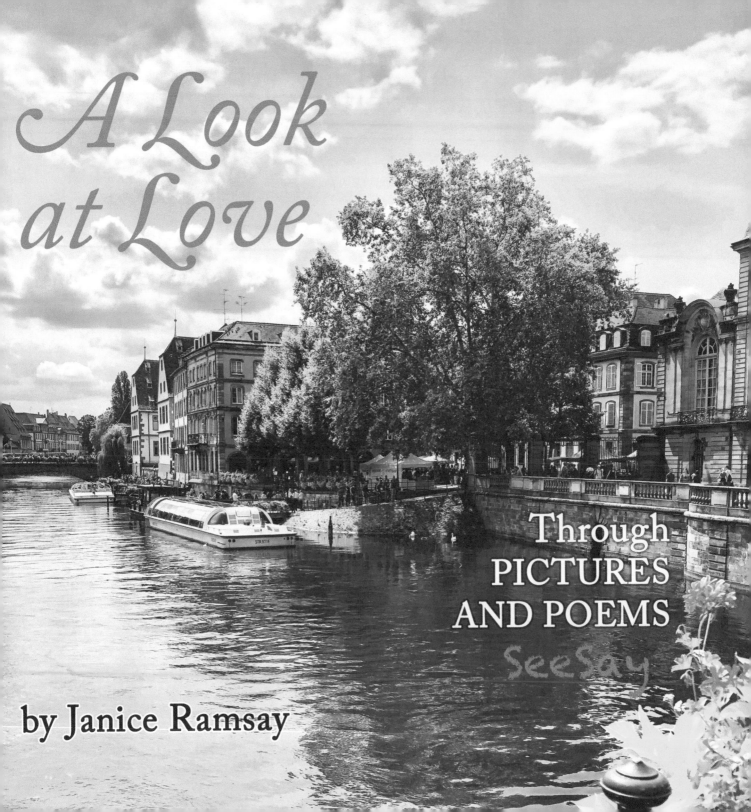

A Look at Love

Through PICTURES AND POEMS

SeeSay

by Janice Ramsay

A LOOK AT LOVE

ISBN: 978-1-952617-66-9 (Paperback)
ISBN: 978-1-952617-67-6 (Hardback)
Printed in the United States of America.

Rustik Haws LLC
100 S. Ashley Drive, Suite 600
Tampa, FL 33602
https://www.rustikhaws.com/

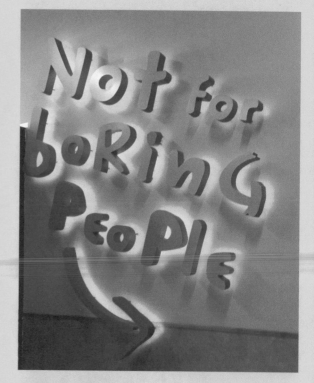

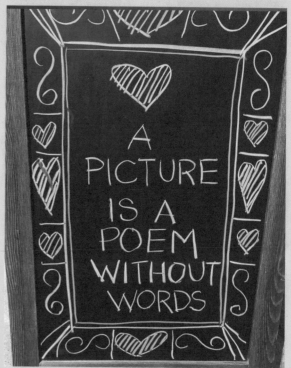

A LOOK AT LOVE

TABLE OF CONTENTS

Is love a work of art or
sailing on a deep sea?

ABOUT LOVE

"Love is not love
Which alters
When it alteration finds…"
by William Shakespeare
Sonnet 116

"I Love You, You're Perfect, Now Change"
Title of a music comedy
by Joe Di Pieto

MORE THAN WORDS CAN SAY

Words are not sufficient

To tell you how I feel.

Oh, I can say "I love you"

But that would not reveal

The bond I feel between us

That time and acts create

To make your place in my life

One that parting cannot erase

And though we all separately

Must find our destiny

Our love for one another

Is quite enough for me.

BECAUSE YOU'RE MINE

I love you when the day starts
And in the sun or rain
I love you when the day ends
When you feel good or pain

I love you when you're busy
And when things are kind of slow
I love you when you're dressed up
Or just in comfy clothes

I love you when you play or work
You're gentle and you're kind
I love you when we disagree
I love you because you're mine

STILL TOGETHER, WHEREVER

The pictures of the two of us
I love to have and show
Should be a strong reminder
No matter where you go
That my love is always with you
On each and every day
Whether you are near me
Or very far away

But please don't fly too far away.

IF I COULD ONLY TELL YOU

If I could only tell you

The joy your love gives me

If I could only tell you

How good our life will be

If I could only tell you

Just why you make me glow

And why wherever you are

Is where I want to go

If I could only tell you

I would and you would know

How much you mean to my life

And why I love you so

NEXT TO ME

I want to feel you next to me
In our cozy bed
I want to put my arms around you
And my head beside your head
I want to feel our bodies touch
And keep each other warm
And spend the night in blissful peace
Until we see the dawn

HEARING
YOUR VOICE

I love to hear your voice
From any source at all
A message on my voice mail
Lets me know you called

I love to hear your voice
When we are on the phone
No matter what you say
I know I'm not alone

I love to hear your voice
When you are next to me
Your voice gives me pleasure
Whatever the words may be

I love to hear your voice
When we are tucked in bed
A whisper that you love me
Are the best words ever said

BUILDING LOVE

Can love be as tall as buildings
That are several stories high?
Can love be strong as archways
Built in times gone by?

Just how does one build love?
It's difficult to say
I have heard from others
You must build it day by day.

Put each brick in one by one
With careful thought and care
Each one will test the mortar
That all of them must share.

If there is an earthquake
Turn the debris into art.
Overlook the small cracks
Throw the rubble off the cart.

And if you help each other
And build with love and care
You'll find there is a stairway
To a LOVE that's always there.

A LOVE BIRD

This little bird
Was found on the bed
The hotel maid
Had shaped its head
She added flowers
And with a twist of her hand
Gave the towels
A way to stand.

Now I know that
Love is believed to be
Only the sort
That couples see
But I would say
There are other kinds
That this special bird
Brought to our minds.

A stranger showed us
Loving care
We looked at this bird
And became aware
That this effort
She put into our room
Was a love that made
Our spirits bloom.

LOVE IN THE MORNING

Do you love me in the morning
When my hair's a fright
When I creak with each step
After the long night?

Do you love me in the morning
In my quiet fog
When my head is slow to think
And all the world's a bog?

Do you love me in the morning
Before I take a shower
Before I put on makeup
And I don't smell like a flower?

Well, if you love me in the morning
When all these things are true
I know our love is more than courting
And I can count on you.

AIRLINE LOVE

From the first time I met him
I knew he was FIRST CLASS
He seemed to be all BUSINESS
So I thought I'd have to PASS
His love came at a PREMIUM
I would have to CARRY ON, too.
I did. So he's my SEAT MATE
And we're each others CREW.

LOVE AT A DISTANCE

You are very far away
Unlike here, it's night not day,
I know you must be sound asleep
In a slumber, oh so deep.

I think of how my sleep will be....
It's warmer when you're here with me.
I like to hear you breathing deep
Your breaths a steady rhythm keep.

I long to cuddle again with you
Waiting a week will have to do
Until then, have peaceful dreams,
I'll see you when the full moon beams.

SWEET DREAMS, MY LOVE

LIFE WITH YOU

Life with you is wonderful
What more can I say?
To be with one
Who cares for me
In so many ways
Makes every day
That comes along
Seem like a treasure chest.
No matter what I take out
I know that it's the best.

Can love be a treasure chest?

THE ROSES

A dozen red roses
Arrived here today
I knew it was love
They were meant to convey.

The thorns were all gone
From the stems of the roses
So I would avoid
The pain a thorn poses.

The love they conveyed
Was stronger than words
For words can be lost
In air like the birds.

The flowers you gave
Like our love, grew in stages
The memory of their beauty
Will last through the ages.

Caution

Walk slowly
at this elevation.

MOUNTAINS OF LOVE

I'm breathless, yes, breathless,
And in love once again.
I'm looking at love's highest peaks:
Where does the climb begin?

The mountains are so beautiful
Seeing them can change my day,
But I've tried mountain paths before
And boulders blocked the way.

Can I step around the rocks this time?
Climb up and bear the winds?
All love in life has obstacles
Some have discouraged me, but then…

I have seen the joy I radiate
If I can can climb and stay.
I gaze again at the peak and sigh
Yes! This time I'll find my way.

THIS EVENING'S SUNSET

Today I watched the sunset

And admired the evening sky

I know this happens every day

And so I wonder why

This particular fading sun

Gave me an empty sigh.

Could it be that you're not here

To share the evening's lore?

All sunsets have their beauty

They're something I adore,

But when you're here,

Their beauty seems, to mean

Oh, so much more.

BEING BESIDE YOU

Being beside you
Is as good as life can be
A hug, a kiss, a touch from you
Are all wonderful to me.

So as you roam the earth, dear one,
No matter what you see
Remember that true love awaits
The next time you're with me.

IT'S MORNING

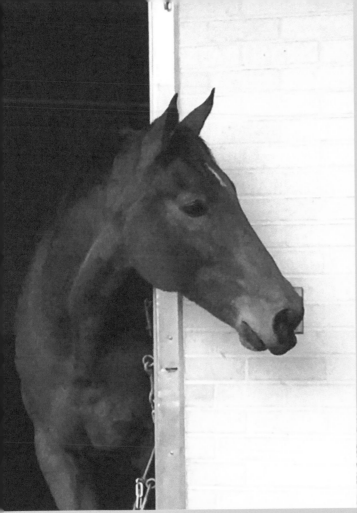

It's morning and as usual
I am up and all about
And you, my dear night person,
Who falls asleep upon the couch,
Are still under the covers
And happily in bed
With a couple of fat pillows
Tucked under your dear head.

So I will use this quiet time
To think sweet thoughts of you
And cherish our life together
No matter what we do.
Nothing is forever
And I know that life is fleeting
But I can love you tenderly
While my heart is beating.

31

REMEMBER DARLING, JEWELRY PREVENTS HEADACHES.

DIFFICULT MOMENTS

Sometimes I find relaxing
A difficult thing to do
I know that such a problem
Does not challenge you.

So I find ways to calm myself
You may not understand
They don't change my love for you
Or the joy of holding hands.

My need for you grows greater
With every passing day
I never like when we fight
And I can only say:

"Please forgive me when I hurt you.
It is not my intent.
Your are the most important gift
That life has ever sent."

TWO INDEPENDENT PEOPLE

Sometimes it's hard to please you
No matter what I do
And I know, from what your've said,
That you feel that way, too.

We've both had the experience
Of being on our own
And find that too much "mothering"
Is smothering and groan:

"Please let me do it my way"
And I guess that's what will be
Each of us is stubborn and
The other's way can't see.

But in time I've realized
That our differences are small
And fade in their importance
When we see things all in all.

So I'll try to just let go
And let you have your way
I want to show you that I care
By what I do and say.

LOOKING AT YOU

I love to look into your eyes
And see your lovely face.
I love to listen to your voice
And fill our time and space.

May it be with joy and laughter.
But even when you cry
I always want to be with you
And help you wipe your eyes.

I want to show you that I care
And make music for your ears.
So tell me what makes you smile
And how to please you, dear.

For the moments that we share
Are the sweetest I have known
And I want to reap the harvest
Of the seeds that we have sown.

CATCH A RAINBOW?

If I could catch a rainbow,
I would do it just for you
And share with you its beauty
On the days you're feeling blue.

If I could build a mountain,
You would have your very own
Place where there's serenity
And time to be alone.

If I could know your troubles,
I would toss them in the sea
And you would laugh and smile again
And sing a song with glee.

But I cannot build a mountain
Or catch a rainbow from the air,
But I will be what I can be:
A friend who's always there.

The Joy of Holding Hands

HOLDING HANDS

Do you know how much
I love to hold your hand?
A squeeze between our fingers
Is like a heart drawn in the sand.
It communicates so much to me
Though it's quickly washed away
It tells me "you and I " are "we."
On this and other days.

Moments like these that we share
Show what a touch can say.
My heart knows that you LOVE me
In so many ways,
So I keep that thought inside me
As I go throughout my days.

A SPECIAL LOVE

We each long for the day
When we don't have to fuss
To get another to love
All aspects of us.

Sometimes such a love
Is hard to find.
Love is a quilt
With many pieces to bind.

But when a special love
Does come our way
On what otherwise might be
An ordinary day

Or even at a time
When we've stopped caring
There comes that moment when
Someone is daring

To look our way
With a noticeable longing
And, suddenly, we feel
A sense of belonging

With that special person
Who loves who we are
Then our days feel so lovely
And as bright as a star.

IT'S QUIET HERE

It's quiet here without you
And though quiet can be nice
Without you standing
Somewhere near
Life seems to lack it's spice

I can't wait to see your face
And ruffle your scattered hair
I want to feel your arms
Around me
And feel how much you care.

I'll be glad to make your cup of tea
And butter your burnt toast
Please let me be
Beside you soon
It's your love I cherish most.

LOVE has

SOME HIGH FLYING and
SOME HARD LANDINGS

I'm in love
Let's just take off
We will fly away
All will be ok!

Could things change
When we get off the plane?

Guess we'll see
Won't we?

THE SEASONS OF LOVE

Love in the spring
Seems to sparkle so bright
We think it's forever
It glows in the night

Love in the summer
Can be awfully hot
When the heat gets intense
We may untie the knot

Love in the autumn
When leaves fall to the ground
Can make us have questions
And look all around

Love in the winter
Can have highs and lows
We can be warm or cold
During life's winter snows

Although the seasons of life
Will have their day
Love still brings us together
In its own special way

I WONDER "WHY"

You relax with your love
And enjoy a day
But some doubts keep getting
In the way.
Love can give you choices-
To stay or to go?
You wonder "Why?"
But really don't know.

When you get too near
It feels a bit strained.
The reasons aren't clear
But you feel a bit drained.
Is it time to explore?
To walk out the door?
You wonder "Why?"
But stay for more.

You know there is no
"Happily ever after."
You try each day
To have some fun and laughter
But there may be a time
When you need to cry.
You wonder "Why?"
And so do I.

Is love like a cuckoo clock?

Does love take setting the table right
or some careful watering?

LOVE and LISTENING

Sometimes I find listening
A difficult thing to do
I think that I'm too busy
And don't concentrate on you.

Then you feel neglected—
I don't mean for that to be…
I know I feel the same way
When I think you don't hear me.

If love is based on listening,
We all have a lot to learn
To give another the attention
For which we ourselves may yearn.

"Is not within our nature"
Some of us will cry
But there are some experiences
That cannot be denied.

So maybe, if we listen
To what another has to say
When we hear, it may appear
That love will come our way.

WHAT LOVE CAN DO

I feel so taken care of
By your loving ways
Like a baby in the womb
I trust in every day.

Like the bird that's flying
Way up In the sky
My wings have air beneath them
That lifts them way up high.

Like the fish that swims
In the salty sea
The water keeps me floating
And swimming far and free.

Like the flower that's growing
In a deep moist soil
I keep feeling nourished
Without excessive toil.

Your caring love's
A windmill that I know powers me
It makes my life so happy
And flow along with ease.

**Like the flower that's growing,
In a deep moist soil**

About the Author

Janice Ramsay wrote the poems and took the pictures in this book. Jan's working career has been as a lawyer and as an expert witness, but she has always expressed her own creativity in various ways and enjoyed the creativity of others.

A later in life romance, some of which took place at a distance, gave her inspiration for writing poetry. Digital photo technology and travel prompted her interest in photography. She has combined them into what she calls **"SeeSay"**—See the pictures; Say the words and ENJOY the feelings.